Having Lived

Having Lived

Poems by

Joseph Murphy

Kelsay Books

Cover design: Shay Culligan
Cover Image: istock Ronda Kimbro

ISBN: 978-1-947465-79-4

Kelsay Books
Aldrich Press
www.kelsaybooks.com

For Winnie

Acknowledgements

Adelaide Literary Magazine, "For Emily," "Your Footprints," "Comrades"

The Ann Arbor Review, "Learning to Dance," "In Marshall"

Ambassador Poetry Project, "Memorial Day"

Civilized Beasts, "What the Cat Thought"

The Driftwood Review, "The Straights"

Earthborne, "The Robin"

The Externalist, "Greensky Hill"

Falling Star Magazine, "Shooting Star"

Flutter Poetry Journal, "The Convent"

The Four Seasons Anthology, "Black Ice" (Kind of Hurricane Press)

Grasslimb, "Lost Coast"

Loch Raven Review, "After a Fire at A Jewelry Store"

Northwind, "Hull Down," "Big Mike"

Open Thought Vortex, "Star, Stone and Blade," "A Star"

Poetry Quarterly, "The Journey," "Whitcomb Summit," "Night"

River Poets Journal, "Winnie"

Circle Show, "Doris"

Sugar House Review, "Back on the Island"

The Tower Journal, "Black Jack"

Third Wednesday, "Birdland Baby," "At Sea"

Umbrella, "To Horace"

Vanilla, "Becoming Kim," "Danny Boy"

Vox Poetica, "The Desoto," "One Long Night," "That Summer Storm"

Westward Quarterly, "O Life"

Willows Wept Review, "The Storyteller"

Your Daily Poem, "Father and Son," "Seaside Farm"

Reference

José Emilio Pacheco, 1997. *City of Memory*, trans. Cynthia Steele and David Lauer. City Lights Books, San Francisco.

Contents

About the Author

It's best to believe that everything happened
as it should.
And to be left in the end
with a single certainty:
of having lived.

—José Emilio Pacheco

Black Jack

I wonder if you lived to celebrate a new millennium.

Grandmother knew only that you had fallen
when a scaffold broke apart.

I hope the bricks you last laid are still in place.

By the time I was adopted
by one of your 13 children
two world wars had come and gone.

You, a family legend: Boston Irish, first over, 1852.
Dark hair and dusky skin
sparked a nickname: Black Jack Murphy.

You sized up your share; took it
by luck or cunning; a fit patriarch,
jabbing or dogging
until a way could be found.

No kin has matched your storied verve.

What of that other tale passed down?
Your father stealing sheep; fleeing
from Spain to Ireland; thus, your Moorish coloring.

What of his famed Robins'-egg-blues eyes?
Enough to turn that Irish girl's head?
Had she come to love a thief
unknowingly? Willingly?

I wonder if she lived to see you set off.

I picture your hand releasing hers; she in prayer
as your ship neared the horizon; you on deck,
facing the open sea.

The Convent

For Victor de Perez

A bed for them had been a narrow plank: for a pillow,
a piece of wood we'd stack by a fireplace.

I hoped the reward for such contrition
had been sublime.

Their mummified remains stood in open coffins
leaned against a cellar wall. Dressed in coarse habits,
they had likely sewn, eternity for these nuns
included being displayed
to disbelievers.

We passed through quickly, in silence:
better to endure insult or loss
than hard truth at an arm's length;
better, still, to stride a broad Mexico City street.

What a fine noise
rose from that bar we found,
where workdays ended; what a delight
to laugh in that crowded,
smoky room.

The Desoto

The 10-year-old sat up to see over the dash,
imagining the engine's sound.

September 1959: shuttered summer homes;
gift and soda shops closed; the island's beaches
reclaimed by gulls.

The car had been sold; time to move.

This would be his final chance
to marvel at its dials.

Death had come quickly: Grandmother
walked in, saying, "He's gone."

The boy had come to see himself
as a figurine
glued to a bottled ship's deck.

But sitting in the driver's seat
he seemed life-size:
holding the wheel's worn grooves,
just as another had.

After a Fire at a Jewelry Store

That he had gone unnoticed seemed miraculous.

How much longer
could he poke among the ashes?

Where was that dream-sized jewel? His share.
Was it to remain imagined? One more hope
soon to burst, its shards
hollow as moonlight?

For that soot-covered man, better the hunt
than to linger in the square;
better to risk arrest
than to lack.

Better yet, and easier, by night
to scoop coins from a fountain,
taking what others had wished away.

But this was a singular chance.

Don't we each harbor that greater end: a find
that can transform us?

So, more power to him! Let him pocket
his life-changing prize.

Back on the Island

1.

The crowd, the glare, the clatter:
those first hard, fine moments;
a sharpening of loss.

Ashore, heat and clamor. Flushed,
fumbling, I must pause;
regain my footing.

Oh, just keep on; walk, head up; just breathe.

Soon enough, I'd soften, slow.

So much the same: eave and gable; hot
pavement; souvenir shops
brimming with goods.

Not all the oaks still stood, though,
along Penacook Avenue.

2.

Near the wharf, I leaned upon a railing
where a young man once had,
that day he judged
time had come to leave.

Passers-by, who noticed, saw an older man
gazing at the sea.

3.

I tried to retrace
that track I followed west,
the one I had thought
so well marked.

Much I believed would matter hadn't,
though some lines held.

4.

Noon on the island: breezy, cloudless;
I would sunbathe and swim
until the evening boat arrived.

Heading to the beach,
I noticed a boy
struggling with his downed kite.

I showed him one way to get it back in the air.

Hull Down

I preferred to swelter in the pilothouse,
than brave a flying bridge
at noon near the equator.

I'd pace away another watch:
binoculars lifted, lowered, lifted again;
strap weighing down
a soaked collar.

But that day another vessel
rode the horizon,
momentarily,
shape distorted by distance and heat.

I imagined myself on that ship
sighting ours:
as skewed by sky and wave;
as remote.

Shooting Star

1.

We neighbors gathered in the park that night
to watch Sputnik cross our sky.

The first to see pointed, drawing all eyes up
to that singular light
rising above oak and eave.

Moving swiftly, surely, Russia's star soared past.

2.

An 8-year-old boy imagined
it had shaken free of its orbit; looped and pitched
above a steep-peaked roof, gable and porch.

He saw it loom larger, faster, brighter.

Sharpened by the strop of space, he watched it cut
limb from maple; root from loam.

Just then, grandmother smiled, saying, "Let's go in."

The boy who took her hand looked back,
still tracing that orbit.

He saw it graze the counters of a kitchen
where she had first held him;
spin down a lane where she had once reined-in
a hay wagon's spooked horses;
swoop along the edge of her father's fields
where Indians had camped

that Canadian spring.

For him, it flared and skipped
past stone and shell; through his out-stretched arms,
toward the jetties, the sea.

Greensky Hill

1.

Would the dirt road's tight curves be too much?

Foliage pelted the windshield, caught in wipers;
the squeal of limb against metal,
again and again.

But the annual Hemingway tour
was not to be disrupted:
our bus soon ascended
that hill he had taken in a buggy.

2.

We'd lunch as he had
at the Horton Bay General Store:
that boy among boys,
bright with stories to come,
surely as hungry as us.

We'd pause by a circle of trees
the Ojibway held sacred,
near Peter Greensky's church.

Sitting in the pews,
we'd hear of a girl from the tribe, Prudence Boulton,
whose father had been a sawyer
for Dr. Hemingway.

She'd soon come to covert his handsome son;
and as he once wrote,
the good taste of her mouth.

3.

Behind the church, I found a path:
I'd follow it up through a wooded knoll;
down and past well-tended graves.

I'd see emblems carefully set
in remembrance of veterans.
Small flags, too: honor, duty.

Many, though, had been forgotten:
their graves marked by
weathered epitaphs and crosses
slanting from the brush.

4.

Returning, I'd overheard this: "She's buried here."

Prudence. I hadn't known.

Pregnant: 19. She'd committed suicide,
as had Richard Castle, the boy she'd loved.

Her unmarked grave seemed part
of an untended garden.

A patch of petal and stalk was bordered by stones
pushed unevenly into the loam:

One of the ladies on our tour
knelt down to straighten them.

Learning to Dance

Aunt Florence always began each lesson
with the box step.

The waltz didn't seem quite right
for me or my time:
but I'd smile, try again.

Left foot here, right there: cha-cha-cha.

I'd need to relax, learn to lead, she'd say,
as she led me
to and fro.

Upstairs, I'd close my door
hoping she wouldn't hear the radio
or me stomp about, as I tried to imitate
how the older kids danced
on American Bandstand,
certain I mostly looked silly.

We hadn't yet heard of Saigon or Hanoi;
didn't yet dread the evening news.

We could still focus on the sound of thirty-threes.

Music on, with Mrs. Dowdy's hand in mine,
we'd foxtrot: Flo on the couch,
laughing, approving.

Lesson done, I'd head to town, play pinball;
ride the Flying Horses,
hoping to grasp that elusive brass ring.

By the time I'd return, she'd be lost to gin.

The only time I saw joy in her
was during those lessons,
and I'd never let her down.

With the volume up and chairs pushed back,
her arms steadied mine
as I edged forward.

Seaside Farm

For Lauren

One photo captured the breadth
of that Alaska of hers:
a broad, sloping meadow
wooded at its far end; the distant bay
framed by a snow-capped range.

With it came a remembrance:
the scent of ocean and evergreen
carried on a well-felt breeze,
as I caught my breath at the top of a hill.

She wrote of bounding from a cluttered van;
tumbling into the tall grass
of Seaside Farm's wide open;
laughing, somersaulting;
friends at her side.

My sixteenth summer
was shaped by island and beach,
rarely beyond a bicycle ride
from family or town.

She'd chosen to tent beneath the midnight sun,
savoring the far off.

She'd return home, though, this time.

The Storyteller

1.

I endured the downpour
as I leaned against a eucalyptus,
pondering my willingness to hike
without regard to weather.

I could cut back through the tall grass,
getting soaked to my knees, or take another slosh
though muck.

Either way offered an easy fall: I stood fast.

An elderly man came up, whistling.

The surf was high, he said, well worth the walk.

He told the story of a king
who had drowned
after commanding the breakers
to part before him.

Remember that, he said.

Not to be outdone by a man his age, I pressed on.

2.

Standing by the sea,
I wondered what fable I'd recount
when my turn came.

I didn't want that story
lost to weakness or weather.

I wanted my listener to heed, walk on.

Birdland Baby

You described a comfortable apartment:
clean, reasonably priced; a friendly place;
perfect for a young lady
new to post-war New York City.

But you'd prefer to remain silent:
drawing the story out
took patience.

You'd dawdle, but finally admit
late one night you'd squeezed into an elevator
with Lester Young and friends.

That lonely first Thanksgiving,
you sat on the window sill wondering
why you had ever left Natick.

Then, the bell rang.
Smiling, Billie Holiday invited you up:
if, that is, you'd help cook.

Cutting vegetables, you worried her ash
would land in the gravy, smoking and talking
as she stirred the pot.

In fact, a mix you'd simmered
back on North Main Street
was being served.

Your astonished father had burst out,
"You listen to too much
of that goddamn jungle music!"

But how could a jazz fan resist
palling with Mingus, Dizzy and Monk?

Night after night, Birdland: Pee Wee,
the midget who ruled admittance,
grew so fond of you
he waved you in, free,
no matter how long the line.

And on your birthday in '51,
the party was stage-side, Miles Davis
buying your drinks.

You and he were sitting close by the cake
when a photo was taken: For nearly 50 years,
you'd keep it
in one wallet after the next.

But before returning to Natick,
you cropped him out.

At Sea

I paced the flying bridge.

Dawn: only my watch awake;
clear, breezy.
heat still bearable.

No scent or sight of land; no other vessel.

Our bow cadent: lifting, lowering;
cutting ahead.

Easy to imagine
none had set that course;
come that far.

Becoming Kim

1.

He always seemed the odd man out:
the son who never measured up; the lesser brother.

He did gain a fair share of attention:
the piranha in his fish bowl;
the German Shepard he commanded
in what German he knew, "Schnell! Heinz! Schnell!"

No other family member drove faster;
had fewer passengers.

2.

Rumors began to circulate.

His mother refused
to finance the operation; he threatened
suicide.

She collapsed at a bus station, one story went,
sighting him in a skirt.

3.

My cousin, decked-out in a denim jumper,
nylons and heels,
offered me a holiday hug.

A new name had been chosen: Kim.

Scenes from a shared youth
unraveled; so many
missing pieces.

Here stood a new being: fearless, poised.

Smiling, Kim spoke of a real past:
sneaking into the attic
to don his sister's clothes.

No more!

Fit to be seen; scarred,
but the riddle solved; mascara
healing the wounds.

Lost Coast

1.

The narrow dirt road's steep curves kept us in first.

Too much dust
with the windows down; but too hot
rolled up.

Redwood boughs sprung at hood and fender.

The Beatle revved, jolted forward:
growled, strained, as if a harness
gouged its neck.

I thought we'd soon be walking.

But hazard seemed a required course
that summer of '68.

2.

Parked and shouldering packs,
we welcomed the open of a sandy meadow;
joined long-haired companions
camped by a stand of alder.

Cattle grazed on the hillside; steelhead
sought the river's shaded pools.

We gathered driftwood and watercress,
dozed in the sun; quick only
to voice an opinion.

Blunt, outspoken,
each offered a greater truth,
unaccustomed to regret.

3.

Exulted by wine, each evening
we'd walk the beach.

Fishermen worked in moonlight,
using triangular nets
to scoop grunion from the surf.

Camping beneath the headlands, their fires ranged
from candle-sized to pinpoint,
from where we stood
in the haze at the mouth of the Usal.

4.

Darkness freed us to lie on the sand;
perform that time-honored scene
penned by our ancestors;
lines rendered with a sigh.

5.

Years later, I found our campsite:
bluff overgrown by nettle.

I knelt where steelhead had darted
before the drought.

Walking that riverbed, I recalled
the lives and deaths of friends,
my own haphazard path;
how much I'd come
to doubt.

Memorial Day

The flag remained visible above the knoll,
as if held aloft
by the drummers' cadence.

We stood by a Civil War memorial.

Name, rank and Michigan regiment
marked most graves, though I noticed
"Soldier in the Army" and name
on a number of them.

Some sang or whispered
"America the Beautiful," others
simply moved their lips,
suggesting an incantation.

Returning, I took a lane
down the cemetery's border,
a green in clear view.

The course seemed especially lush:
golfers motored past in carts,
clubs neatly bagged.

The Robin

Newly plowed fields leant me their brilliance.

The breeze hailed furrows in my wake; churned
through flower-haze
and noon's heady brine.

But a robin dove
to bumper height; struck; cart-wheeled
into the brush,
emptying my hands.

Star, Stone and Blade

For Victor de Perez

1.

He spoke of bow-hunting pheasants
amid the sugarcane and sage
near Cuernavaca.

I thought we'd be hiking the plain.

But he'd chosen a steep, dusty path
through boulder and weed:
"Surprise," he said,
"this is Xochicalco."

Workers lunched beside unearthed walls;
a stepped pyramid's stonework
began to emerge.

He led me to what seemed a cave at its base.

In flashlight-illuminated coolness,
the hollow grew smaller, hand-cut.

I clicked off the flash in a domed chamber:
a sunlit circle
appeared at our feet.

Elders had knelt on sacred cloth,
a polished black stone
before them.

Torches extinguished, moon and starlight

fell through shaft
to stone: movements marked;
a calendar set.

2.

Beyond the broad plaza, wooded hills.

A serpent god towered above us,
coils sculpted
across a temple's sides.

Lingering by an altar, I imagined
the rite: blade hafted; wrath forestalled;
tracks of moon and star
maintained; harvest
assured.

3.

The trail down
crisscrossed tops of blocks; a half-buried terrace.

Dusk took hold; night while driving.

Our headlights
cut a short, but steady path.

The Straits

I felt the ship slow as I readied for watch.

After so long at sea: a jungle's scent;
the sound of breakers.

Clouds obscured the moon as I took the conn.

Ahead, fishermen slept in unlit skiffs,
some near the channel's center:
gray hulls faint on a deeper gray.

I rocked them in our wake:
calm enough that night;
no jolt, no cry.

Doris

1.

She smiled as she pushed along:
still using her walker; still at home.

Frail, beautiful, the former model
greeted me with a kiss.

A boy then, she was the first I saw ill.

Polio had struck in her late twenties; before 35
she'd be bed-ridden.

I visited the hospital once.

She offered a smile,
but her words were slurred, high-pitched,
agonizing to hear. Shortly, anger
overwhelmed her. She flailed her arms,
in tears; my uncle,
hand on her forehead,
tried to calm her.

2.

While she could still sit on their porch,
I had helped him plant hollyhocks,
as she sipped tea.

The tall flowers still remind me of her
and summer evenings
I spent eluding dragonflies
as she looked on.

The Journey

It was late; lost.

I'd passed
the same fast food joint
again and again;
upscale theme-eateries
and retail outfits
appeared to reappear
at will.

I kept changing radio stations; nothing soothed.

Finally, the right set of turns. I rushed
to unpack, get out,
walk.

The hotel edged a strip mall,
its vast parking lot
empty.

Amid well-measured spaces,
I watched the moon
clear dense clouds.

In Marshall

The news is not good: refugees huddle
in a muddy field. Channel surfing,
I'm drawn to their story,
again and again.

Like me, many in jeans; jackets
with a team logo.

Many in traditional dress
had survived a similar dread
when young.

I had left family and familiarities
without fear: traveled cross-country;
19-years-old; exhilarated.

Setting down the remote, I set out
to walk our quaint,
Midwestern main street.

Seeing my reflection
in a store's window, I'm shaken
by the finality
of lineage and chance.

O Life

I could feel it as ever
as I ran those empty, still-dark streets:
that full-stride link
of muscle, heart, breath;

glad to have gotten out;
put strength first.

A certain headiness
surfaced from the smoothness of my pace:
but a skull, spray-painted
on a concrete slab
hit me hard.

"O death in life," Tennyson writes,
"the days that are no more."

But I ran on: still as fit
as ever; another finish line
to cross.

Father and Son

For Jonathan

Startled by the crash of surf,
my 4-year-old son said, "Be quiet ocean."

He gripped my hand: sand on lips, teddy bear,
hot dog and crushed bun; new clothes
tattered; sneaker lost;
cheeks streaked war-paint black
from driftwood and grime.

He smiled. I clicked.

Later, with him snug in a sleeping bag,
I hiked a steep hill above our camp.

He woke as I stood at the top, raising his arms
for me to lift him. I could hear him calling,
though he was thumb-sized.

He stopped crying after I'd held him for a while.

I knew I'd need to remain in reach
until his fears receded.

The Star

I'd never met another on that steep hill's summit.

Wild flowers grew as they would
along a country lane: sunset
highlighting petals.

I stood on jagged rock, vastness
of skyline and bay below.

A star appeared through sheer clouds: that instant
the past seemed no more
than an empty page.

For Emily

In Remembrance

It seems your years were set too closely together:
when one toppled, all the others fell.

Shut the power off, you said. Enough. Your body
quickly shut down.

Your smile is now as ours will be:
a few to recall, then none.

No trumpets, no drum roll: a short ceremony;
then on to spring, to summer.

Thousands had died the day before: an earthquake;
mud-brick houses.

But it was you who brought death into focus.

Outside and alone, fists clenched, sunlight
seemed to jab at my bent neck.

I began to breathe deeply: arms back; chest raised.

I was sure I could push
my heart beats aloft, hoping your spirit
might gain by it.

I don't know why I did this, but it mattered.

I'm still trying to reason it through:
but the parts keep changing shape,
falling from my hands.

Winnie

1.

Grandmother said it was because of the Southerner:
He had broken something in the girl's mind.

That born liar: threatened marriage or suicide;
she was too young; confused.

The coward even came north.

No one heard, rose: he shook her awake;
bluffed, pleaded;
smooth-talked her into the car;
rolled it to North Main.

He took her to the bayou: pregnant, miserable;
that cruel son-of-a-bitch;
that's when it broke.

That's how grandmother put it.

2.

1940: Winnie likely tapping her foot
to a Dorsey Brother's tune.

His sister might read her latest poem;
or, tired but exhilarated,
discuss that evening's dance contest.

Ten years later, Red Sox on the radio,
the phone rings; Allen answers.

It was someone from a veteran's hospital.

When he reached Brockton,
he couldn't see her.

Everyone hoped
one shock treatment
would do.

3.

I found a box in Flo's garage
filled with her things:
a poem published in a Boston paper;
her photo, in uniform; short stories,
hand-written in a high school notebook.

I was in my early teens; had no idea
where she might be.

I had seen her at a bus stop that winter:
stood back; got out of sight.

Her hair was uncombed;
a torn coat worn over an ill-fitting dress.
She was loud, way too loud;
other women nodded, tried to be polite.

I hid. Waited.
Could she really be my mother?

4.

She escaped again and again;
would find me.
I remember her slouching
on Norman's couch:
forehead in hand, smoking a butt
picked from the ashes.

"Don't worry," she said.

5.

Laura said Frank
drove Winnie to Lafitte
in his Model T, down Bayou Barataria's
lone, shell-paved road.

He had met her near war's end:
she, a Navy nurse; he, a wounded Marine.

Laura said Frank got spooked by loud noises,
had lunged beneath a kitchen table.

She thought it had to do with Guadalcanal.

Laura spoke of Winnie disappearing
night after night.

One morning, Frank could take no more:
he found her with my 2-year-old sister and me
beside an abandoned stretch of track,
ready to board.

6.

I was 20 when I saw her that last time.

She smiled proudly; introduced me
to each nurse on her ward.

She was determined, the three of us
would be reunited: her, my sister and me.

She would get us a cottage; white with yellow trim.
She would fix us up: had the money,
just needed more time.

What kept going wrong, I asked.
What was it?
I wanted her side of it;
finally, had the courage to ask.

She looked off, saying, "Sometimes,
I just get the blues."

That was it: the blues.

Black Ice

Sleet obscured my view; bent me
toward the wipers' drone.

None ahead or behind.

My bright world right
to link will to a well-known machine
asserted.

But I swerved—breath held—the tires bit,
yanked me back.

White lines, asphalt
reappeared; I could hear
the radio again.

Comrades

The two were depicted on posters
hung by the door.

Lenin, 8-feet-tall, wore a dark cap, suit and tie;
red ribbon on lapel.

Pravda peeked from a vest pocket: the truth.

Facing the kitchen, chin held high,
he looked past it:
confident those below had heard his call
to press onward, ever onward.

The man-sized Santa doffed his cap:
magnanimous, smiling, list in hand;
another entry made.

And so they hung, paper-thin, until
late one night...

Dream transformed them into an apparition:
hammer, sickle, harness and sleigh
swirled above me.

Clattering, clanking, bellowing, they battled on
until, in a final whirl of color and light,
the images dissolved.

I woke clenched to pillow: the hued, crisp air
of the still hushed city
calmed me.

Up, blinds raised, I cracked an egg
to sizzle in a black iron pan. Coffee made,
toast buttered: It was time.

Two specters came down: manhandled
from wall to trash.

What the Cat Thought

The sharpest edge
could never pierce
as do my eyes.

I leap, lie in the sun,
lick the dust
from my lovely paws;
stretch, purr.

Ah, what fangs!

I banquet
on the meek's
tiny bones.

Beware!

Whitcomb Summit

1.

It seemed the cabins could be felled by a breeze;
lawns, paths and flowerbeds
had given way to meadow.

The tower stood
as an empty parking lot's centerpiece;
a hand-painted sign
cautioned 50 cents was due
before ascending.

A small fee
for that sweeping view of the Berkshires,
last seen as a boy.

2.

I'd traveled the Mohawk Trail
with my uncle, "Jitterbug Murphy,"
as he was known
in Boston's pre-war dance halls.

I wanted my son to see
one of the places
we'd been.

3.

In my boyhood, I'd admired
photos of the long-legged beauties
posed in dreamy allure

on B-29 noses; learned gremlins
caused engines to smoke; imagined myself
as a pilot-warrior
poised to fly "over the hump."

4.

He was too short to enlist.

Norman won't quit; kept getting in line.
Finally, the Air Force said yes.

He wrote home from Kansas,
Panama, Guatemala.

No torpedo would thwart him: he slept on deck
all the way to India; on Tinian,
stopped his Jeep short
to glimpse the Enola Gay.

5.

Remembering the pluck
a rubber tomahawk had lent to hand,
I paid to climb the tower.

Catching my breath at the top,
I began to wave to my 12-year-old son,
but he had fallen asleep
in the car.

Danny Boy

Success seemed inevitable in '65,
every street Easy Street.

We'd be seen cruising Sudbury
in his Austin-Healey: young men
going a bit too fast; top down; relishing
the stir; the envy.

Our future
seemed as simple to grasp
as the pop lyrics
swirling in our heads.

But success proved rock-candy-hard.
It chipped teeth
on the way down; stuttered that long stride
we'd taken for granted.

When drinking, drugs and binge-eating
tore at his heart, regret wasn't enough.

The handsome cousin I'd idolized
collapsed in his mother's arms, dead at 47.

But those songs? The promise? Short on nectar
and long on shadow; shards
littering a narrow track.

Our elders' kindness had proven unkind.

The Depression. Soldering
through a world war. Why speak of either?
or ballistic missiles? the Berlin Wall?

So much to be kept
from a child's reach;
so much to shed.

But we needed harder lessons.

Standing up was to be a gamble,
not a sure-footed certainty.

It turned out a head-long fall
would always remain
a step away.

And it wouldn't be a fall
into reverie or love, but a tumble
from the edge of a honey-coated world,
as if from a tower
into a drained pool.

That Summer Storm

For Kirsten—in remembrance

The thunder woke me.

Lightning's blue flash
colored the sill; rain
cooled my bare chest.

I joined friends
after a bolt
shot through pine
yards from where I lie.

We huddled in a narrow stairwell.

The children joked;
giggled.

My knees shook at each peal:
too dark
for them to notice,
luckily.

Big Mike

1.

His wholeness came from muscle tone, endurance:
a body willed to shape; refined daily.

The best workout the hardest: worth defined
and redefined; strength as bliss.

His features mirrored Hemingway's Paris years.
His presence emboldened me: offered the flair
I lacked; the verve.

Together, we'd press through La Gloria's
swinging doors. Tijuana at rock-bottom best: Tequila
poured in tall water glasses; ear-shattering salsa;
a drunk passed out at the bar's curve;
fist-fighting locals
vying to pay the prettiest girl
a few pesos for a dance.

Ah, but for you, señor…

Another adventure
spent in his shadow: no qualms,
once we safely returned.

2.

The change came quickly.

He had lost the benefit of the lightest of metals,
lithium, that soft, silver-white torch.

His thoughts broke loose; collided.

As heavier elements descended, he chose to write
his own prescription: in a good-natured delirium,
found his way to Key West.

But he was in retreat: strength soaked out;
he replayed that Ketchum scene,
completing the likeness.

3.

When I got the word I had to get out:
couldn't speak; reply.

I worked to stay on my feet
that cloudless day.

Your Footprints

1.

Was it '42 or '43?

You, on liberty in Miami:
off watch, wandering from beach to bar;
cast from destroyer grey
into a bright colored world, Massachusetts
a snow-bound memory.

But what of this shore leave? The last?
what might flash brightest at life's end?

What better for a young man:
the memory of a woman.

Ah, that fateful dance at the USO:
Kitty as war bride
three weeks from first sight.

Your screen-test-perfect features,
hale build, warm grin,
arm slung over a shipmate's shoulder:
that photo said it all—
Adonis in Cracker Jacks.

Miss Miami never had a chance.

But love didn't survive
that collision of desire and war.

You: Boston-Irish; smooth talking;

but hard-nosed, hard-drinking;
hard-bitten by the depression, hungry to succeed.

Her temperance and Baptist virtue
didn't fit. Your fears didn't help.
The soft-spoken beauty queen
seemed too easy a target.

Your motto: keep her barefoot and pregnant.
And the custom was marriage, no matter the cost;
neither ever rising past anger to peace.

Subterfuge. Neglect. Late in life, two fighters
would be led from the ring: dazed, bloodied,
but separated at last.

2.

You would return to Miami,
manage a swing band:

Forty-plus years since liberty call had last sounded.

We'd meet. Our fighting days done:
not a word about Vietnam.

You played me a tune
the band had played.

3.

On your death bed, just audible,

you said you were proud of me.

I told you I loved you,
set down the phone and cried.

But what to add? Subtract?

As a long-haired, Sixties teen, I didn't suggest,
I proclaimed; unequivocal.

Vietnam, simply a starting point. I'd persist,
asserting a litany of your wrong turns.

I'd surely avoid them—no question, Alan, I'd win.

Now, I'm the age you were then: hair graying;
no less burdened; no better off.

As a young man, I thought I could navigate
by the stars of my choice.

Now, I take a shorter view. My aim:
the horizon, one step at a time.

It's no surprise
to find your footprints
at my feet.

One Long Night

The wind wouldn't relent
that night the rain ended.

Redwood tops tossed
as did I, unable to sleep.

Sight of a sheer white beam
too close to ignore
focused my angst.

I bolted up! Pitched
toward the window...

My opponent: the moon,
splinted
by swaying limbs.

To Horace

You told Dellius he would die,
regardless of how well he had shaped his world.

But the gods held you in higher esteem: no death
for your voice, though your shade
long ago boarded that darkened boat.

The incense and music you knew
still rise from page to life—fresh cut lily, rose
and blossom-of-parsley
welcome us as we join you
at Numida's return.

Of course, the wine still flows.

Gathered on a beach near Tarentum,
it's your grave we've found, not Archytas'.

It's you we hear when the sailor cries out.

But we've not come
to mourn: the finest part of you
has outweighed death.

Your voice still colors the Hyperborean steppes.

No need for three more handfuls of sand, either,
to ensure Fortuna's blessing:
your songs remain sung.

To celebrate your gifts, they'll be no stop
to the dancing. Bring more wine! Offer Horace
raised cups, a garland of myrtle; like him, marvel
at what Clotho has spun.

The Navigators

The buoy rang steadily
as I walked glade and redwood grove,
that free day of mine.

I paused in a meadow, eyes closed.

Bell in my heart,
be heard as clearly:
guide me
and those I love.

Envoi

A Letter

For Richard Tillinghast

You are one of the few who will remember
late spring mornings on Walnut Street;
those adored sisters.

The distance to Maurya's fingertips
seems no greater than to this line's end:
but only with eyes shut.

Stanzas seemed to come so easily then.

But what joins word to world
can easily break, can't it?

Years later, walking Walnut Street,
I wasn't certain what I would recognize.

I began to wonder if I had ever come that way.

But you had pushed ahead: line by line;
the able one, year after year; each word
perfectly aimed; no unraveling.

I never imagined I could begin again,
but whatever was broken
has healed.

About the Author

Joseph Murphy is a retired public relations executive. His poetry has appeared in a wide range of online and print journals. Murphy's first collection of poems, *Crafting Wings,* was published in 2017. Murphy attended high school at Tabor Academy, Marion, Mass. He went on to earn a bachelor's degree in comparative literature from the University of California, Berkeley, as well as a master's degree in human resources management from Golden Gate University, San Francisco, Calif. While at Berkeley he was awarded the Eisner Prize for poetry, the university's highest award in the arts. Murphy is a member of the Colorado Authors' League and for eight years (2010-2018) was poetry editor for an online literary publication, *Halfway Down the Stairs.* He is also a veteran, having served on active duty and as a reservist in the U.S. Navy, retiring as a commander.

www.ingramcontent.com/pod-product-compliance
Lightning Source LLC
LaVergne TN
LVHW021621080426
835510LV00019B/2687